SCARRED
FOR LIFE

SCARRED

Stabbed 39 Times and FORGAVE

FOR LIFE

A true story by Fredric A. Almond, Sr.

TATE PUBLISHING & *Enterprises*

Published by Tate Publishing & Enterprises, LLC
127 E. Trade Center Terrace | Mustang, Oklahoma 73064 USA
1.888.361.9473 | www.tatepublishing.com

Tate Publishing is committed to excellence in the publishing industry. The company reflects the philosophy established by the founders, based on Psalm 68:11,
"The Lord gave the word and great was the company of those who published it."

Book design copyright © 2008 by Tate Publishing, LLC. All rights reserved.
Cover design by Stephanie Woloszyn
Interior design by Kellie Southerland

Published in the United States of America

ISBN: 978-1-60604-581-7

1. RELIGION / Christian Life / Inspirational
08.10.31

Dedication

First, to my big brother, Joseph L. Almond: You have been my life line; because you live it causes me to continue in living. You have been there for me in the hard times.

Your love for me has been my inspiration to keep moving forward. Your example has caused me in not giving up.

Secondly, to my spiritual big brother, Elder Sheldon O'Guinn: You have always provoked me to do good works in challenging times. We have been together in ministry over a decade. When I wanted to let go of the calling and run away, you encouraged me to continue on in breathing. You showed me why it was important to breathe and for others to live. You were the iron that kept me sharp and focused on God.

Thirdly, to Apostle Harry and Cora (Mama) Das: You both have been a great inspiration in me living life. You have always treated my family and I as your own blood family. I always knew that your prayers were there for me for protection from the attacks of the enemy and in pressing toward my accomplishments and fulfillments of attaining my prize in Christ Jesus. Never once have you doubted what God can do in my life. You both have helped me in allowing God to reveal the gift of God that has been placed in me for the nations. Your examples and passion for Christ have convicted me to refuse defeat but to walk through it with joy.

Fourthly, to those who have been scarred physically, mentally, or spiritually: Your scar is only positive fuel to move forward. You are alive because God has more life for you to live. It's people like you who are needed to be used as strength for others to overcome. I hope this book is one of many that will launch you out in the deepness of God.

Acknowledgments

God has chosen me to do a work that is for nations and for that reason, he has placed very vital personnel in my path to keep me focused and motivated. During these particular times, they were the ones who I drew strength from and leaned on for encouragement. They empowered me with words of hope and motivation that God is able to do the impossible.

I take this time to give God thanks for all of those who have been there to remind me to keep my aspiration toward Jesus Christ. You have given me the determination and inspiration in my life. Because of this reason, I can't let you all down. I give special honor and recognition to:

- My wife, Rose Marie Almond, whom I love with all of my heart. Your continued love for me has been my inspiration to be all I can be. It wasn't always easy to understand me, but you never gave up on me. Through our struggles and difficulties it has made this marriage complete. There is no other woman for me; I love you with my whole heart. I appreciate you and all that you do.

- My four blessings: Danielle, Gabriella, Elizabeth and Fredric Jr., whom I would die for. You are the apple of my eye. I hope that my successes will be stepping stones for greater success in you alls life. I constantly pray that there will be something that I do on this earth that will cause for you all to be proud to have me as your Dad. You mean everything to me.

- My big brother, Joseph L. Almond, who had to bear my pain while ignoring his. You were there in my weakest, struggling, and hardest times. You had to accept the roll of a father at a young age while you were still learning how to be a man yourself. Your unselfish actions developed a conviction in not giving up.

- My Father, Frederick J. Masey and brothers, Johnny, Tommy, and Noah. Through the years, God has truly reconciled our relationship. It was the power of God's love that healed the hurt areas and brought us back together. I thank God for you and our relationship.

- My Aunt, Shirley Gillium, you've always made sure that I am being properly taken care of. You always go the extra mile in putting a smile on my face. Your example of love has showed me that it doesn't take lots of money to show love, but it takes love in action.

- My cousin, Ellis Bradley, you were the forerunner of introducing me to Christ. Your motivation and passion for God gave me that same attitude. Words cannot express the appreciation that I have for you.

- My family, who I wouldn't trade in for the world.

- My spiritual family, who have been the extra determination in accomplishing the task at hand. You would not let me give up and provoked me in doing good works. (Elder O'Guinn, Deacon Franklin, Deacon Jackson, and Brother Thomas and their Families.)

- Shirley Bogan (my spiritual big sister), who had to be a mother to me. I'm sure you didn't know exactly what I needed, but you trusted God. Your boldness, persistence, and spiritual warfare tactics are still within me today.

- Apostle Harry and Mama Cora Das, my spiritual Father and Mother; you both mean so much to me. Your covering is what I needed to launch forward with humility. You have kept me from getting stagnate and kept pushing me for excellence in love. Your example is what has caused my family and I to emulate Christ more.

- All the pastors, their ministries, and the relationships with the saints that have sowed seeds into my life. I will always be indebted to you and have you in my heart. You are the success in my life to get to the next level in God.

- And to all of those that I didn't name, Thank You!

Table Of Contents

Preface

Fredric Almond shouldn't be alive, a veteran homicide detective will tell you. Instead, he should be a casualty—one more murder statistic chalked up to the violent neighborhoods of South Los Angeles.

Sheriff's Sgt. Jerry Jansen was sure the 11 year-old son of Alma Almond would die on Sept. 4—the day after Labor Day. The youth, stabbed an estimated 30 times, was in surgery as the detective entered the well-kept home where Fredric lived with his mother.

The body of Almond, 33, was on the living room floor. She had been stabbed more than 50 times.

"That house was one of the bloodiest messes I've ever seen," said Jansen. "It's not often you find two victims in one place who have been stabbed 80 times between them. It was almost like a shark going into a frenzy.

"It's a miracle Freddie survived. We didn't think he would ever get out of critical care. He was critical for two weeks. I don't think I have ever seen a stabbing victim live (after sustaining) this much damage."

Kenyon said that no motive for the attack has been determined.

The "miracle" in Fredric's recovery was that none of the knife thrusts hit a major artery, according to Dr. Lonnie Smith, one of the surgeons who worked on the youth during more than four hours of surgery.

"It took a lot of work to repair the injuries he had," said Smith. "I would say being young was in his favor. But still, there was a good chance he wouldn't survive. His trachea was pretty well severed, so the main risk to his life was asphyxiation."

There's also a chance he may never regain his ability to speak.

But the doctor says he seems to be healing well in other areas, where the scars might run deeper.

"Overall, he's a pretty strong kid," said Smith. "The trauma of watching his mother stabbed, and being attacked himself would be a lot for anyone. We thought he would need some psychological counseling, but he's handled it real well. Other than some periodic depression—which is understandable–he hasn't really needed regular counseling."

Now 12, Fredric seemed to be healing well from his wounds, though his neck is lined with thick scars, when he was visited by a reporter Friday. Gauze, wrapped inside the collar of his rugby shirt, obscured most of his throat and the opening of his tracheotomy.

He was able to make himself understood—mouthing words and, at times, almost whispering them—but he was generally limited to one-word responses.

It's the little things that give Gillum hope that Fredric is going to make it back all the way from his tragedy. Her nephew, she'll tell you, is a survivor.

"We haven't talked that much about what happened that night," said his aunt, "but, one time, I asked him why he didn't die. All he said was, `I didn't die because I didn't want to die.' "

Said Leslie Kenyon: "He's a brave kid. Not because he testified, but that night, after being stabbed that many times, he was still trying to get help when he collapsed. And you don't think there are heroes these days?" [1]

Introduction

I write this book in gratefulness and dedication to my LORD and Savior, Jesus Christ. If it had not been for Him in my life, I wouldn't have made it this far! I am indebted to Him for the rest of my life and will live a life that will express my gratitude for all that He has done for me. I truly didn't know what life was all about until death came knocking on my door. Through a death experience, life came. It came in a way that I had to make a choice whether to live or to die. Choice is a very powerful tool that is not always used properly. There are times when we choose life but it doesn't happen the way we desire it, and we wish we could take it back. However, the reality in my choice to live produced many scars. One may ask, "Why choose life if it's going to produce scars?" I realized through my experience that scars are *testimonies that give us fuel to move forward.* Many people live their lives in circles never overcoming their scars because they chose it to be too much for them to handle. In other words, the wound never fully heals because the choice to live in action is never accepted, it's just like picking at a scab, not allowing the hurt and pain of the wound in being properly healed.

A scar is meant to cause recovery. The process of recovery will cause something different to be experienced in our lives. However, we don't always accept recovery. Full recovery causes us to perform in ways that we don't always believe that we are ready and capable of handling. If I only knew when tragedies were coming, I would think that I would be better prepared to handle it. At times, I preferred not to wait for the recovery because the process felt like it was taking entirely too long. My concerns were, "How long do I have to go through this" or, "Why me" or "Now that I have these scars in my life, what do I do now?" These concerns as well as others have caused many to give up on living life in expectation and hope and ignored the reality of the experience of recovery. We get so used to the happy ending story, but happy doesn't always come the way that we expect it to come. Sometimes you have to fight for happiness by it producing a scar. Yes, it's okay, you have a scar. Your scar is what makes you special. Have you ever thought what having a scar means? These are a few infallible proofs of what God has made you to be with the scars that are in your life:

- *Shaped in His image.* "I praise you because I am fearfully and wonderfully made; your works are wonderful, I know that full well" (Ps 139:14, NIV). What makes you beautiful is being able to see your beauty in God when you have been scarred.

- *Unashamed to be selfless.* "For whoever wants to save his life will lose it, but whoever loses his life for me will find it" (Matt 16:25, NIV). You are willing to go through embarrassments, pain, and hurt to cause recovery for someone else to live.

- *Flavored to live life.* "Salt is good, but if it loses its saltiness, how can you make it salty again? Have salt in yourselves, and be at peace with each other" (Mark 9:50, NIV). Keeps you at peace in spite of what you have been through due to your scar.

- *Overcomer.* "I have strength for all things in Christ Who empowers me [I am ready for anything and equal to anything through Him Who infuses inner strength into me; I am self-sufficient in Christ's sufficiency" (Phil 4:13, AMP). Being able to encourage yourself and believing that this too shall pass.

- *Determined to recover.* "Brothers, I do not consider myself yet to have taken hold of it. But one thing I do: Forgetting what is behind and straining toward what is ahead, I press on toward the goal to win the prize for which God has called me heavenward in Christ Jesus" (Phil 3:13–14, NIV). Regardless of your past hurts and failures, you remain focused on remembering what your future beholds.

- *Willpower.* "For God did not give us a spirit of timidity, but a spirit of power, of love and of self-discipline" (2 Tim 1:7, NIV). Equipped to face life's obstacles even when it may seem scary

- *Living and walking in victory.* "He himself bore our sins in his body on the tree, so that we might die to sins and live for righteousness; by his wounds you have been healed" (1Peter 2:24, NIV). Through His sacrifice your scars have been healed for purpose and have given you the rights to live in freedom.

- *Scarred for life.* But he said to me, "My grace is sufficient for you, for my power is made perfect in weakness." Therefore I will boast all the more gladly about my weaknesses, so that Christ's power may rest on me" (2 Cor 12:9, NIV). Your scar is not weakness for life, but strength to fulfill your destiny.

The reality of facing life's challenges may take years before it becomes a permanent scar of fuel to move forward. While going through this process, we must accept that God is allowing a scar to be produced. You are somebody; yet, you may have this scar in your life.

The purpose of a scar is to fulfill the identity of who you really are. However, scars don't occur in order to dictate you as being worthless or downtrodden. When we understand our true identity of our scar, it will cause a greater conviction and determination to fulfill our purpose. Scars permanently absorb the hurts and pain of the experience. It is meant to be a reminder to be looked upon as strength; the same God that brought you out of other situations is the same God that will bring you out of this one. How long will it take for reality to kick in? It's time to face your obstacles head-on! My experiences have made me stronger and have given me a greater perseverance and a press to attain what was promised to me. Though it is not always easy, you must refuse to give up. This scar that you may be facing is what's causing you to live. It's now time to use the scar for what it's worth, living life to its fullest!

Lifestyle

While growing up in the heart of Los Angeles, California, I had to grow up learning the "streets." It was always about respecting the environment or knowing about the "set" that I lived in. Dangerous times would be present in certain neighborhoods based on simply the attire that was worn, looking too long at someone, or even walking down the street alone. Moreover, there were times when it didn't matter if all the precautionary measures were taken; problems still occurred. In order for me to survive, I had to adapt to the environment while making preparations for my future. I had to understand where there was a safe haven and where there was corruption. As a child, it seemed like corruption was a part of my life a lot. I lived in an environment of drugs, prostitution, theft, alcoholism,

imprisonments, gangs, mental and physical abuse, etc.
Corruption seemed to be a way of life. Mom tried her
best to keep my brother and I away from corruption,
but, at times, it was unpredictable. Because of this reason, we had to stay alert and be ready to react at any
given time. One may be tempted to think that this is
not fair and feel they are authorized to complain about
the way life is. Though we go through these challenges, know that God is developing us in being stronger in Him. *If we could turn in the hand that God dealt in
our lives and simply get another one, it would be so much
easier,* we think. We have to be careful that we don't
allow disappointments and discouragements through
complaining of what and how we believe things should
happen in our lives. Regardless of what type of environment we live in, we are able to overcome it and make
a difference. No one said that we have to be like the
environment we live in. Though we have some misfor-
tunes while living this life, God is still under control.
Yet the environment we live in is not always enjoy-
able; we must guard our heart from being persuaded
into thinking that we will never overcome the struggle.
We must stop ignoring the issues, acting like nothing's
happening; we must begin to face them. Our lifestyles
are not dictated by society. We are left to decide if we
are going to make a difference in the life we live. We
can easily be locked in life's challenges, never overcoming our trials. What keeps us locked in from the challenges we face are scars of insecurities and fears. These
two are good friends, and they tag-team against others.
These two friends live and abide in the neighborhoods

we live in. Their purpose is to gang up on us, always trying to prevent us from moving on. They strive on influencing us in such a way that it keeps us afraid to go down the road of challenge. If these bullies are tag-teaming in your life, making you feel unprotected or believe that you are not strong enough to handle it, I must remind you that there is nothing too hard that we can't handle and overcome. It's now time to be brave and put your belief into action. "No temptation has seized you except what is common to man. And God is faithful; he will not let you be tempted beyond what you can bear. But when you are tempted, he will also provide a way out so that you can stand up under it (1 Corinthians 10:13, NIV)." There is nothing that is able to have a grip so tight that it can't be released off of our lives. God will never let our trial be greater than our ability to stand through it. As a matter of fact, once we begin to understand our trials are stepping stones to guide us toward our purpose, it takes the sting out of the trial.

We must *believe that God can* work things out even when it seems impossible and in spite of what the challenge may bring. God allows trials to happen when He knows we are well-equipped and capable of handling the situation. He expects us to use what He placed in us. God doesn't give us strength for us to run away from the problem. No, He allows for us to go through it to help show us and others that we have victory over the trial. If you didn't go through any trials, how could you be an effective encouragement for someone else who is presently going through what you've already came out of?

Our struggle to enter through the door for freedom is not only for our welfare of making it through, but it is to make a lasting impression for others to follow through it. Someone is depending on you to set the example.

You are blessed; you have been given the antidote by God to be strengthened in the midst of sufferings and pains. Don't allow your life to be mastered by the environment you live in, but master it. This is a fight that you can win. This fight is not for your life only, but for someone else's as well. You have been given what it takes to be an example for someone else in how to fight as an overcomer and win through the hurts and sorrows that occurred. You may be the only or last overcomer for someone else to remember what God can do in their lives. Stop making excuses and looking for pity about what hand God dealt you in your life. Remember, you have what it takes to be effective. You are blessed not because of the situation but because God says you are.

Acceptance

I must say, I am one of the many people who wasn't brought up in church. Therefore, I had no experience or understood who Jesus was. My church experience was during Easters when I would get a new Sunday suit from JC Penny's or Montgomery Wards. I remember sitting in the pew being tired, bored, and ready to go home. The words that the preacher spoke seemed to go through one ear and out the other. Other than that day, I knew nothing about God. I thought that people around the age of sixty or older would go to church only. My initial plan was to make it rich and live a lavish lifestyle to its fullest. Then at the end of my journey, I would start going to church. I felt church was only for old people or for people that were ready to go to heaven.

One day, my cousin, Ellis, came over to visit. We

were sort of startled by the excitement he expressed. Our first thought was that he got a new job or someone gave him some money. Come to find out, it was much more than that; he expressed with great adoration that he accepted the LORD Jesus as his Savior at a local church in the neighborhood. It is hard to express in words the excitement and enthusiasm that filled the room. His outward appearance brightened up the house. What he had given me was the desire to get the same thing even though I didn't quite know how or what it took. The change that took place in his life was the final draw in what he received. He literally looked like all the weight of his burdens was taken from off his shoulders. His reaction was a smile of gratitude, of unspeakable joy; it was uncontrollable. As he walked around the house, he began to solicit family members in going to church. Nolan (my cousin) and I seemed to be the only ones that accepted the invitation. His passion and change is what gave us the motivation to go with him. We didn't have a background of church protocol. We just wanted to have what Ellis received.

On Sunday morning, Nolan and I were getting dressed for church. We put on our nicest slacks and collared shirts. We were so excited; it was something new, something different. It was something we never experienced in our young lives. We had the inner assurance that wherever we were about to go, everything was going to be okay. The church was located in the local neighborhood. There was nothing abnormal on the outside. As we entered in the church, we were struck by the atmosphere of singing, dancing, and people shouting,

"Praise the LORD," and "Thank you, Jesus!" They were excited and carried the same enthusiasm as my cousin Ellis did. The place was filled with an abundance of joy. Everyone seemed to be determined and focused on one thing, giving God their highest praise! Afterward, the pastor began to speak. It was with great fire and passion. He reminded me of a father who was concerned for his children, telling them right from wrong. As he ministered, there were key points he gave that even I could understand. However, I really didn't retain too much of the words that the pastor spoke. Nevertheless, the words that stuck out have impacted me for the rest of my life. By that time, it was close to the end of the service. The pastor asked the question, "Who ever desires to accept the LORD Jesus as their personal savior, let him or her come." My heart froze, not knowing what to do; I felt paralyzed. I wanted to go up toward the front, but my body wasn't agreeing. As the pastor continued to converse, I was nervous. So, I tried to ignore him, but his words were loud in my spirit. I couldn't run away from it. I couldn't do anything to stop the loudness of the Word of God being spoken into my life. I could literally feel the words that the pastor was saying within my soul. The words he continued to speak made me have the assurance that if I were to accept Jesus in my life, I would be protected and looked over. This was a vital time in my life, and I took it very seriously. I didn't want to leave knowing I had the opportunity to receive Jesus Christ in my life. For some, tomorrow never comes and then it's too late. This was my opportunity of accepting Christ in my life, and I would not allow my thoughts to dictate the leading of God in receiving Him. It's easy to lose our opportunities of acceptance when we begin to ponder in our minds that we aren't worthy enough—when we feel we've done too much sin or feel we aren't old enough. All we have to do is accept Jesus in our lives. Don't make it difficult; keep it simple, and let God handle it.

As he continued to speak, I began to reminisce about the joy and new love that my older cousin had felt. I thought, *if God could change him, then God could change me.* Yet being nervous, I took a deep breath and began to walk toward the front. The closer I walked to the front, fear and nervousness of what to expect began to fall off, and I began to be at peace. I sensed an inner strength which assured me that I was doing the right thing. Moreover, I accepted the steps in receiving the LORD as my savior. To ensure that I understood what was happening in my life, one of the clergy showed me in Scripture:

> That if you confess with your mouth, "Jesus is LORD," and believe in your heart that God raised him from the dead, you will be saved. For it is with your heart that you believe and are justified, and it is with your mouth that you confess and are saved" (Romans 10:9–10, NIV).

And that's all it took; through confession of my sins and my belief in Jesus Christ, immediately I was saved! There was such an inner peace that caused me to believe that I was secure and protected. Furthermore, I now was more determined and ready to face my future obstacles because I had Jesus in my life. He rescued my life by giving me the gift of salvation only by accepting Him. There was no better decision that needed to be made. My first test was fast and easy: accept God in my life. I was reborn and better prepared with life in front of me; I was now ready to make a mark for God. Yet, I never knew that I was going to be tested in such ways at an early stage of my salvation that would either cause for me to live or die. I would have thought this gift that God gave me would receive the opportunity in maturing and developing me first. If it were up to me, I would have rather waited a little while before having to deal with certain trials in my life at such an early age. I realized, sometimes we think we are not capable enough and are too young to go through hard problems because we just got saved. Once He comes in, His power abides in us and changes begin to happen immediately.

God allows for us to go through trials and tribulations that we may accept them as opportunities for Him to make known, He has everything under control. These opportunities are forerunners in pushing us to use what we have already received to overcome the situation. Trials are meant to be received as opportunities that are transformed into becoming a testimony of overcoming life's challenges. God will use us in times when we may feel weak and vulnerable. He has a way of doing things that produces the best out of our lives in the most technical, painful, and hurtful situations. God just wants us to trust Him. When the time comes to go through our trial, we are already prepared and equipped because of receiving this impartation of His salvation. When we may say we are not ready, He says we are. We are equipped with everything we need in order to overcome and conquer our trials. This is the place of fertility, a place where the richness and productiveness of His Spirit reveals itself in its most pure form in our lives. In this place, we depend on Him with all our heart, mind, soul, and body. Many times we don't know or understand the potential that we have in us unless we are tested in such a way that cause us to pull from the power within to be released and helps to overcome. Had I known what type of test that was coming, I would have reneged and not gone home that night. I probably would have said, "I'm not ready yet. I need another confirmation. I'm not ready. I need more time." Or, I would have ignored God, never facing the direction of purpose God was taking me. He was taking me to a place that made me more than what I thought I could ever be. Are you afraid to face and go toward the place God is trying to take you? He's doing it to prove that you have more in you than you may see in yourself. When we face our purpose, it will be scary. However, we can't give in to our fears based upon what we see. In other words, what causes us to fear is not knowing and not understanding what to expect in our lives because sometimes it may seem like we are going to suffocate and die in a hard situation. We will not die if we continue to believe in life. Moreover, death doesn't come by sight; it comes by acceptance. Today, what is your choice?

Moving in Your Gift

"Wherefore I put thee in remembrance that thou stir up the gift of God, which is in thee" (2 Timothy 1: 6a, KJV).

It was 1984, Labor Day weekend, a week after I received the LORD as my Savior. Mom was coordinating with the family in coming together to celebrate the holiday. Normally, on Labor Day, we would go to a park and bar-be-que, play games, sit, and laugh. Mom took the initiative by arranging everything that was needed for the picnic as she normally would. She was the chief cornerstone of the family. Mom had a special gift of keeping the family together. Even though she would stay up late at night, organizing and setting up for the holidays, it was enjoyment for her. Her gift of keeping the family together is what pushed her through the tiredness and stress of life's issues. While she prepared, her gift gave her enjoyment. She allowed her gift the opportunity to live. Her gift is what gave her the inner strength to continue on. Our gifts are what give us the edge to overcome our weaknesses. The gift is a spiritual endowment from within that is placed in us before we are even born. This gift is strong and powerful. It can't be destroyed by any trial or tribulation. As a matter of fact, it does its best work while it is in the midst of trials. The gift normally shows up in times and areas when the body feels as if it can't go any further. Moreover, this gift pushes us ahead to become a conqueror and causes us to become more than a conqueror. By the time the big day had come to pass, her gift is what already made the picnic successful because she refused to allow anyone or anything to stop her from accomplishing her mission. Her gift is what pushed her initiatives into a success for the rest of the family.

Labor Day was the last holiday before school started. We made sure to finish the summer out with a blast! During these barbeques, there would be various types of food: grilled chicken, ribs, steaks, hot dogs, hamburgers, sausages, baked beans, potato salad, etc. There was always more than enough food to go around; it was as if we were at a smorgasbord eating all we could eat. The best part of the food was the deserts: banana pudding, cakes, pies, etc. On that day you might want to wear the type of clothing that stretches or fits loosely because you were going to put on a couple of extra pounds. By the time the sun began to set, we would be sitting around talking and laughing about the past, present, and future

things to look forward to. These picnics were thera-
peutic and relaxing. It was as if we were on vacation
far away from our problems. Our best times were when
we came together as a family. Mom never looked for
recognition. Her acknowledgement was seeing all the
smiling faces and appreciation of joy within the family.
Her gift is what caused the satisfaction. These picnics
were talked about the whole year. Times like these were
what kept us sane. The gift that we have in us should
be able to impact other lives in such a way that it would
cause strength of not giving up.

Purposed to Survive

"This was so that, by two unchangeable things [His promise and His oath] in which it is impossible for God ever to prove false or deceive us, we who have fled [to Him] for refuge might have mighty indwelling strength and strong encouragement to grasp and hold fast the hope appointed for us and set before [us]" Hebrews 6:18 (AMP).

As the moonlight shined through my bedroom window, I laid in my bed, staring at the light while smiling. I was now satisfied and ready to go back to school. I began to ponder on all the wonderful activities that I just gone through during the day. I thought in my mind, *I had enough fun to last until next summer.*

It was now time to go to the next phase of education; it was time for junior high school, starting in the seventh grade. I imagined what the new school (Henry Clay Jr. High) would be like and how the kids would treat me. I had my new dark blue Levis and a new thick white t-shirt to wear. Plus, I couldn't wait to meet the girls. It was so hard to go to sleep.

As the night continued to move forward, I continued to toss and turn. That night, it was as if God poured an abundance of joy all over me. I had an assurance that nothing could take away my joy; it was different from any other time from before. Eventually, I began to get very tired and I fell asleep with a smile on my face.

Suddenly, during the night, a scream came from my mother's room; again, another scream that seemed to be louder than the first. Immediately, I jumped up out of my bed and dashed toward the loudness of the scream. I ran into the room, and there was a man that stood about six feet tall in the dark. He seemed to be of a slender build, approximately 180 pounds; he was in my mother's bedroom. I could not see who it was in the darkness, but I noticed the knife that was in his hand. Terrified, I saw this man overshadowing my mother as he began to stab her. In shock, I screamed with a loud voice. The scream startled the man and he turned around and began to chase me with the knife. As his back was turned toward my mother, she began to charge him in defense and protection for my life. He turned back around and began to stab my mother relentlessly over and over again as she kicked, fought, and screamed in desperation. Not thinking, I ran to get help and ended up in my closet in my room. All of a sudden, I began to cry out and pray to God. I didn't really know how to pray because I wasn't brought up in church, but I prayed what I felt in my heart to pray. *Our greatest prayers are the ones that are unrehearsed and genuine, only coming from the sincerity and desperation of our heart.* I prayed and cried over and over again saying, "Help us, LORD! I don't want to die. Help us, LORD! I don't want to die!" I prayed and cried with such intensity and agony. I prayed until something happened. I wasn't concerned about the way I looked or about my age, but I was determined for God to hear my prayer because I knew that only He could save me out of this tragedy that I was facing. I knew from within only He could cause the impossible of living possible. He was the only strength and protector that I knew to call on.

Eventually, I stopped praying because I received enough strength and courage that I needed to face my worst fears head on. I walked out of the closet nervous but no longer afraid. I could still hear echoes of my mother's screams through the whole house. It was one of the worst sounds I ever heard in my life. There was no television show that could match the horror. However, I tipped-toed down the hallway and looked around the hallway corner to see where my mother was. My head was sticking out, and he noticed my peeking at him. Abruptly, he forcefully ran toward me, knocked me down, and began to stab me with his knife on my back. The penetrations of the knife stabs were deep. However, as I continued to be stabbed, I couldn't feel anything that the man did toward me. It was as if God took me out of my body and made me numb to every stabbing. Furthermore, nothing that happened prevented me to stop believing that I was going to live. Eventually, when he felt that I was stabbed enough, he left me there to die and ran back toward my mother to finish what he started. For a moment I just laid there in the hallway bleeding and weak.

As I was laying in the hallway, I could barely move. I continued to try to see what was going on and tried to do whatever I could do to help. I noticed the phone light and stretched my arm out to grab it and quietly pulled the phone toward me. The phone was still on, so I began to try and dial my aunt and cousin who lived about two blocks down the street. That didn't work, so I tried to dial 911. However, the phone had no dial tone. I tried and tried again but still no dial tone. Meanwhile, I continued to lose blood and got weaker. I had to take a few minutes to catch my breath to receive more energy. After a few minutes, I picked my head up and looked around the corner of the hallway and saw my mother and the murderer in the dining room. He continued chasing and stabbing her as she fought for her life. As I looked, he saw me peaking around the corner at him, ran toward me, and forcefully started stabbing me again on my back, on my face, my arm, and even my foot. My mother, being weak and tired because of the fight for her life, had enough adrenalin to run toward him, trying to distract him enough so he would stop coming after me. He jumped back up off of me and began to go after my mother again. She ran behind the table in the dining room while he was trying to get to her and began to bargain with the man, saying, "If you let me and my son go, you can have anything that you want, just let my son and I go!" The man hesitated for a couple of seconds and thought about it. He stood there for a moment contemplating and battling within himself. Suddenly, with all of his might, he charged my mother with such force she couldn't fight him off any longer. He began to forcefully and repeatedly stab her all over her body. A few minutes later, she collapsed and fell on the living room floor.

She laid there dying, making her last moans. The only thing I could do was just lay there and watch from the other side of the living room. I could hear the sounds of the knife going in and out of her body. It sounded like raw meat being chopped up. I couldn't do anything but lay there, watching, and listening. I heard the last sounds and saw the last of the life of my mother. He had no remorse; he wouldn't stop until she stopped moving. He stabbed her until he was absolutely positive that she was dead. As I looked across the living room at her, my mother seemed to be twice her normal size because of all the swelling from the stabbing. It was too dark for me to see her face; I could only see her shadow. He stabbed her a few more times to either make sure she was dead or because of the rush. Finally, he got up with blood on the butcher knife that he got out of the kitchen, walked past me in the hallway, and went back into my mother's bedroom. I just laid there; I purposely kept my eyes opened to see the whole thing. I figured if I acted as if I were dead, then he would leave me alone; him not knowing that I was actually alive. I laid there as still as I could. I wanted him to believe that I was dead with my eyes open. I learned this trick from the movies that I had seen growing up. I laid on the floor as still as I could.

There was an evil quietness that filled the house. I continued to lie still while looking across the living room at my mother. Her body was there but her spirit had gone on, and I knew I would never see her again. But my thoughts were far from thinking about giving up and dying; I thought about how I would live to see the next day.

I heard the keys rattling and drawers being opened. I assumed he was stealing all the valuables that he could find. When he was finished in the bedroom, he walked down the hallway past me to escape back through the back door where he broke in. As he walked past me, he stopped and stood over me looking at my eyes being open. Because my eyes were opened, he was puzzled. He kneeled down, came about two inches from my face, took his knife, and cut me on my face to see if I was dead or alive. He probably thought that if I were alive then I would have moved, made a noise, or done something that would cause for him to react to finish me off until I would eventually die. However, I stared right into his eyes without a flinch. I didn't have time to be afraid; I had to be bold for life.

At that time I had an inner peace. His tactics did not cause me to be afraid. *I stared with eyes of faith looking beyond my trial and looking into my future, having confidence believing that I would survive.* I refused to believe that my life was over. I refused that, regardless of the tragedy that I was facing, it wasn't worth me dying for. *Though I was in a dying situation, my choice to live continued to be my goal of achievement.* I focused on reaching my goal. I had to fight for life because I had too much life to give out. Life is not worth living unless you have it to give out to someone else. The reason you're still alive is because you still have life to give out. Do not allow the devil to win! Your situation will turn around if you continue to believe. *You are a survivor! With survival there is purpose.* How can we survive unless we have a reason to overcome it? We tend to give up because we forget the purpose of it. We have to repeatedly remind ourselves that we have purpose. It will give us the determination and motivation needed to pass the test. We must learn how to look beyond what we're going through. Tragedy is not a reason for us to give up. It should give us a greater push to make it through it. Once the goal is met, it gives us a stronger confidence and conviction for facing the next trial. Don't give up; get to the point that you are persuaded and convinced you have what it takes to live.

He drove off with my mom's car. As I lay there, death came closer to being a reality. I looked across the room at the body of what use to be my mother. All I could do was lay there on the floor and stare at her, not really knowing what to do. As a few minutes passed, an evil thought began to talk to me in my mind and say, "It's over now; go to sleep. It's over." In other words, the enemy wanted me to accept my defeat, think that my life was over, and agree that it was better for me to quit and to nullify my purpose of living before it truly started. Though life's challenges may look dim, it's still worth living for. As I heard the voice, it began to cause me to get very tired all of a sudden. I began to close my eyes and started to fall asleep, not knowing that I was dying and giving up the fight. As my eyes began to close, immediately the Spirit of God said, "Get up!" As I heard the voice speak to me, the tiredness started to break off and strength began to enter back into my body to get up. The power of His voice spoke life in me, triggering determination. I realized that the heaviness that I felt in my body was not heavy enough to hold me down and keep me from standing to receive the energy that I needed to get help.

"And that about wraps it up. God is strong, and he wants you strong. So take everything the Master has set out for you, well-made weapons of the best materials. And put them to use so you will be able to stand up to everything the Devil throws your way. This is no afternoon athletic contest that we'll walk away from and forget about in a couple of hours. This is for keeps, a life-or-death fight to the finish against the Devil and all his angels" (Eph 6:10–12, MSG).

We have to use what is in us in order to live. God desires to unlock that fighter that is within us all. We have more potential than we credit ourselves to have. It's through His salvation that gives us the empowerment to proclaim our victory in our battles. God will never allow for us to be tested if He didn't believe we could pass it. I was able to get up and walk, moving only by the Spirit of the LORD who was my strength.

Then He gave me specific instructions, saying, "Don't go over there by your mother. Go out the door and get help." I did exactly what the Spirit of the LORD said. I operated beyond what and how my body felt like. Even though I took baby steps, I was able to walk out of the door onto the sidewalk. (Baby steps are needed for our walk in God. Baby steps are steps that cause dependency and persuasion in being able to move forward. However, these steps take more time to get to the place that we desire to go. Baby steps make us think that we aren't moving fast enough to receive the help needed. Through these steps, confidence is being built to continue on. At certain times, we try to walk at a rate that will hurry us away from the situation because it's tedious and we don't like the place that we're in at that time. But God wants us to learn how to take baby steps prior to taking full steps.) I wasn't satisfied until I was able to get to a place where I could receive the help that I needed. There are a lot of people that live life without being properly helped. Many times, we go to the wrong place to receive help. We get tired of the journey that God has for us to go. So, we will begin to reason within ourselves, pondering and contemplating about taking a break. Eventually, it causes us to settle for the shortcut of life instead of continuing on fulfilling life.

I was confident as long as I kept moving. It was essential that I didn't give up based upon how I felt and what I was going through. I couldn't allow my trial to be my crutch in stopping. Even though I could feel the blood dripping off of my face and hear myself wheezing every time I breathed, I couldn't allow it to dictate my future. *(We cannot give up because of how we feel and what we see.)* Every breath that I took caused me to forget about my trial. Instead, it caused me to believe and focus more on getting to a safe haven. This was my way of escape. I was able to bear it because I kept moving on toward my purpose for life. Having aspiration for life gave me the inner strength in refusing to stop breathing and gave me the willpower that I will live. Yet my body was very heavy on my legs, and I wanted to stop and give up. I couldn't, however, because I confidently believed I still had life in me that needed to get out. *(We cannot believe in death when life is present in spite of the challenges we face.)* I could barely pick my feet up to move forward and my head kept falling to the side when I would try to straighten it. Nevertheless, I refused to stop and be discouraged in continuing on. I depended on living, and it was my guide and my motivation. Because I didn't give up on God, He didn't give up on me. I couldn't get into a pity party and get discouraged or depressed. Any deceptive tactic to quit is used by the devil to get us to stop moving forward. Tragedy can be heavy and unbearable, but God is capable of making our heaviest burdens into being light. What may seem impossible to us is possible with God. In order for God to make it possible we have to believe. Through perseverance of believing, I was able to break the cycle of murder in my family. Until then, everyone in my family had been killed one way or another. They never died from sickness or of old age; it was by being killed. My surviving was due to unwillingness to die even though anguish and distress came. Your perseverance will do the same; it will break off things in your life as well as in your children's lives because of that gift God placed in you.

Every movement that I took was being controlled by the voice of God. Encouragement came every time I took a step. I figured that if I could make it to my aunt's house, everything would be okay. She lived about two blocks down the road. However, I didn't have enough strength to make it there. The voice specifically told me to go to the house two houses down. Even though it was two houses down, it seemed to feel like two miles. I began to beat on the door with all my might and cried out, "Help me! Please, help me!" The people were hesitant in opening the door because it was late, and it was in South Central. (In South Central you never know who may be at the door, so you must be very cautious in being polite.) Instead of opening the door, they called the police. After a couple of knocks, I began to get very tired from standing, and I sat on the porch. I was able to rest because I had an assurance that everything was going to be alright. I then knew that I was at the right place to receive the help that I needed. It took the police officers no time to get there. The officers didn't know what to expect. They approached me with flashlights and holding their gun's in the other hand. When they saw me, they immediately called for the ambulance. They were in shock by what they saw and began to secure the perimeter. As the ambulance arrived, I kept falling asleep and waking up in and out. I would wake up for a few minutes to see my surroundings and then I would go back to sleep. I still did not feel at ease with everything that had taken place. The ambulance rushed me to one of the worst hospitals in the city during that time. This hospital was known for not having the experience that was needed and was known for making critical mistakes on patients that were in life or death situations. However, they took me straight into surgery. The surgeons made no mistakes that prevented me from living. It was as if God orchestrated the whole surgery. I was laying in bed after surgery with my eyes slowly opening. The doctor and police officer were discussing about my injuries at the foot of my bed. The doctor said with assurance, "He's not going to make it. He has lost too much blood. In about two hours of time, he is expected to die. There is nothing else that we can do." Then they turned and looked at me, saw my eyes open, and a bunch of police officers began to surround my bed as I was in the Intensive Care Unit. I couldn't talk to them because my vocals were severely damaged. Nevertheless, I had to express myself in a different way besides speaking. Talking is not the only way to express ourselves. As a matter of fact, we have to be able to express ourselves in other ways besides in using our speech. Our actions should be able to speak just as loud as our speech and even louder. When we face challenges in our life, we can't be hearers only, but be doers. Our actions will be the evidence needed as an example for others to use for encouragement. I could not be afraid yet I had to express myself a different way. I had to believe that I was just as effective without using my mouth to get the point across.

In order for the police to go after the murderer, I had to point him out. They had a suspicion of who the person was, but it was important that I pointed him out. The enemy desires to put enough fear within us so that we will not have the courage to speak out against who or what he is. When we operate in fear, we tend to pacify and ignore the enemy in our lives, never exposing him but allowing him to keep us in fear. His desire is to be in full control of our lives. When he is in control, it causes us to live a life of defeat, never finishing the tasks. It is like a person who has great potential, but because of fear, he/she is constantly being hindered of fulfilling the purpose of God in their lives. However, I had to point him out. I couldn't let him get away with what he had done. The book that they presented to me was a book that had a list of juvenile delinquent pictures. It was vital that I operated more in my actions. Words weren't good enough. I had to courageously look and point out the man that had taken my mother's life away and caused for me to be in a life and death situation. Just the fact of having to see this person on a page of criminals was horrifying enough. Moreover, the difference that I had to make was overcoming fear in action by pointing him out of all of those that were on that particular page. The police officers dashed out to catch this man. In addition, my strength was gone, and I fell back to sleep to receive more strength.

I went into a deep sleep, and I began to dream. I saw my mother afar off, and she had her arms wide open to hug me. So I began to run in expectation in giving her the biggest hug that I could ever give her. However, the closer I got to her, the more she began to change, and I realized that it really wasn't her, but it was the devil in disguise. I tried to stop, but I couldn't stop going toward her. I eventually realized that she was not my mother, but the enemy trying to take my life for the final time. After getting close enough to this evil presence, it punched me in the chest, knocked me back and I fell down. I began to lose breath in my dream. Moreover, the dream began to manifest itself into reality. Terrified, I immediately opened up my eyes, and as I battled for breath, no one in the Intensive Care Unit noticed me suffocating. I pushed and fought, but I still couldn't breathe. I was suffocating and none of the nurses noticed it. This was my battle one on one against this evil spirit. Its desire was to stop me before I could get started with the healing process of living. (Many have given up before their ministry started. Fighting for your ministry to live is essential. The devil would prefer you give up and drop dead, because he sees the greatness in you. You must understand what's in you is worth fighting for. You have something that the devil can't have: redemption power to cause change.) Eventually, after a few minutes of wrestling back and forth, the suffocation broke, and I started to breathe again. Due to having the determination to live, I wouldn't give up the fight for breath. Death was in my presence, but I escaped. Even in our weakest point of living, we are strong in God in overcoming the devil's attack. Whatever is trying to stop you from breathing life, don't let it win. "But he said to me, 'My grace is sufficient for you, for my power is made perfect in weakness.' Therefore I will boast all the more gladly about my weaknesses, so that Christ's power may rest on me" (2 Cor 12:9 NIV).

As days passed on, the doctor who conducted the surgeries on me was baffled because he could not explain why I was healing so miraculously. I had too many vital parts damaged; the stabbings cut a lot of it off. Incredibly as it may sound, God began to heal different parts on my body that the doctor could not heal. This is why the doctor gave me the nickname, "the miracle child." When we trust God, it will cause those that don't trust in Him to see for their own selves that God can do the miraculous. God allows us to be put in positions for Him to prove to us He is the same God from yesterday, today, and forevermore. God is still causing miracles to happen today.

Cut to Heal

Healing power is belief plus steadfastness. Healing from internal wounds must be dealt with prior to full recovery. I would have loved to receive full recovery in one day. However, God teaches us how to wait with dependence on Him. Waiting is like lifting weights. In order to maintain the drive to work out, it's going to take time in developing the body. Moreover, waiting builds up our faith and trust in the abilities that God has placed in us. The healing process takes longer when we become impatient. Impatience will grow into frustrations and complaints if we allow it to remain in our hearts. We must learn how to wait. God heals in His timing. In the waiting process, we must understand and believe that God is renewing those areas that were cut even when we don't see it.

I refused to submit to the natural pain I felt; I just submitted to God and believed. It was a simple plan, and I was strengthened daily to continue on with the healing of the cuts. God took every poison out of the cut and reversed the outcome of them and made it into a blessing. When I was supposed to be discouraged, I was encouraged. When I was supposed to be depressed, I was joyous. God healed the cut, because I was willing to wait for it.

God has to put back together the areas of our lives that need change for our purpose. The healing of cuts must be covered properly for there to be internal healing. The outer surface is just the beginning of being healed. Our covering is through our belief in God. We lose proper covering because of doubt. How can God do an internal work if we don't believe that he is going to protect and defend what He allowed to happen? The work within is very detailed. It doesn't matter how one might look on the outside if the inside is all torn up. If the infection of a cut is not covered properly, then the insides of the cut will become infected and will eventually affect our thinking and cause a spiritual disease of hopelessness. We must understand that the cut of the natural is not able to kill the purpose of God that is within our spirits. Nevertheless, if we begin to think that the natural is stronger than the spiritual then we will surely die.

"But he was pierced for our transgressions, he was crushed for our iniquities; the punishment

that brought us peace was upon him, and by his
wounds we are healed" (Isaiah 53:5, NIV).

There are two different types of cuts that take place.
The first cut is to stop or bring to an end of life. This
type of cut is of the devil. He desires to discontinue the
work before it even gets started. His cut is to cause pain,
hurt, fear, and death. The tragedy of suffering through
the cuts was meant to be overwhelming—too much
pain, hurt, and fear. I should have given up and died or
allowed the hurt to be so detrimental that I would be
alive yet living according to the tragedy, never getting
past that day. Death does not have to be breathing our
last breath, but it is also giving up on what God has
set in our lives. We must realize that the challenges we
face are only there to keep us dependant on the LORD.
Cuts that come our way are not strong enough to keep
us down. Regardless of the devil's cut, we are able to be
healed from it. The enemy's cut comes hard and seems
to be such a threat at times because he fears in what
God has placed in us. The last thing the enemy desires
is for us to remember whose we are. This is done by distractions of losing and forgetting what God has already
done. Through our acknowledgement in God, it ini-
tiates His healing power in our lives. How the cut is
healed is what causes the victory over the cut(s) in our
lives. *We must understand and know that cuts will come.*
However, God protects us from the poison of the cut.
Through God's covering, it protects the cut and pushes
out all spiritual infections of doubt. The only way a cut
can't be covered is by losing hope in what He already

promised to do. This hope that we have in Him is able to withstand the hardest tragedies we face. Furthermore, because the devil understands this fact, his goal is to cut and destroy our hope before our purpose is manifested into existence. It's not the cut that causes death, but it's how the cut is accepted. You are still alive because you haven't accepted to give up hope.

When God cuts, he cuts to heal. However, He first has to cut out the bitter areas. God wants to cut out distress, insecurity, un-forgiveness, hatred, anger, frustration, low self-esteem, disobedience, self pity, etc., before He can replace those areas with a heart of courage, inner strength, endurance, perseverance, stability, and stamina. God would never cut something out unless He was to replace it with something better. However, we must learn how to let go, open up, and let God work on us. Through healing, the cut develops into a testimony. In other words, testimonies are produced through the willingness to go through its process of healing. Once this is done, the cut is reversed from being a cut to death and now a cut to life. The cut is now ready to be used as a testimony for others to live. The testimony will grow as it's fed. We feed it by telling others with words of encouragement that they too can be healed from their cuts. We overcome our cuts, trials, pains, and hurts by our testimonies. The victory is in our testimony. Our testimony will cause others to see God. This is the very essence of why we go through trials and tribulation: to receive the reward of overcoming. "They overcame by the blood of the Lamb and by the word of their testimony; they did not love their lives so much as to shrink from death" (Revelation 12:11, NIV).

Cuts that cause scars on the inside are vital. The internal scars that the natural eye may not see are more personal than the scars on the outside. Internal cuts are not noticed by the naked eye. This type of injury often-times is ignored because most would rather not face the proper healing of the cut. Instead, we try to cover it up while still hurting, refusing help from God. We say things like, "Everything's fine," "Nothing's wrong," and "I'm alright." Truthfully, the pain still remains while it's never being dealt with, just ignored. Moreover, we have even tried to make our own solutions of dealing with the pain by reasoning within, "If I let someone know about the cut, it will bring embarrassment and humiliation." The devil desires that we continue to stay in this pit of pity, having the mentality of never getting over it. We cannot fix the cut on our own. We must realize the first step in receiving healing is accepting help from whom God chooses. We must receive His assistance in selecting the best candidate for the healing. Hebrews 11:19 says, "Abraham reasoned that God could raise the dead, and figuratively speaking, he did receive Isaac back from death" (NIV). Isaac had to entrust in his father Abraham in overcoming death. Isaac lived because he neglected his own opinions, feelings, and own ideals and solely trusted in God's way. He believed that he would live and not die. God's way of healing is not always what we think it should be. He uses others to be a part of the process. Our strength alone is not strong enough. In order to receive healing from a cut, let Him come in. Regardless how God heals, know that healing will come. Just believe. God specializes in the impossible. He will mend back together what was ripped into pieces. God will never let us down. God doesn't cut to hurt but to heal.

You Were Beautifully and Wonderfully Made

"I will confess and praise You for You are fearful and wonderful and for the awful wonder of my birth! Wonderful are Your works, and that my inner self knows right well. My frame was not hidden from You when I was being formed in secret [and] intricately and curiously wrought [as if embroidered with various colors] in the depths of the earth [a region of darkness and mystery]. Your eyes saw my unformed substance, and in Your book all the days [of my life] were written before ever they took shape, when as yet there was none of them" (Psalms 139:14–16, AMP).

As I began to receive strength, I wanted to see myself in the mirror for the first time since this tragedy happened. I was nervous and felt like I wasn't prepared to see what I had to see. The truth is that I didn't really expect to see what I saw: the truth in the mirror. I looked at myself and began to cry because I was disgusted and horrified of what I saw in the mirror. There were thick white bandages wrapped around my whole head. My face was swollen with many cuts of dry blood stains on the wounds and the bandages. Some of the wounds still had wet, fresh, dark red blood protruding out. There were large staples in my face pulling back together the skin that was ripped apart from the knife that had been used. The images were deceiving in making me feel like I was the most horrific sight ever, much like the Elephant Man. There were two long scars on each side of my neck. The muscles in my neck were very weak. For this reason, I didn't have enough strength to keep my head straight up. My head would fall to the left or right when I would try to lift it up with all my might. Due to severe damage to my neck area, I couldn't breathe out of my mouth. They surgically placed a trachea in the bottom of my neck until my vocal cords healed enough for me to be able to properly breathe. I overheard the doctor say that my vocal cords would never be the same again. My speech would be very high pitched or very low, but normal was out of the question. My neck was not strong enough for me to swallow. In order to be fed, they placed a tube through my nose to my stomach, taping it against my nostril. Tubes ran from the vein of my hand to different medical equipment. I had all these new scars on my face, arm, back, hand, and foot. I felt like the ugliest child in the whole world. The day before, I had no scars and now I had experienced a total makeover. Could it be possible that this was a nightmare and I had not woke up yet? Could it be that I had died and did not know? To some, it would have seemed like my life was over. *I look so ugly,* I thought. I couldn't bear to look any longer at myself in the mirror. I hated what I had become. I once looked like a swan, and now I had become an ugly duckling; there was nowhere I could run or hide. It was as if I had been forsaken. God wouldn't let me die or run away from this tragedy. I had to face the truth. Even when I may have wanted to give up, God wouldn't let me die, but I had to go through it. I had to face the tears, sufferings, and pain of the truth in order to not give up. Through my weaknesses being expressed to God, He became strong in me. He was the encouragement that gave me that inner strength to persevere to get back the joy of being beautifully birthed and made in His image. Even though my outer appearance was horrifying, He reminded me about the joy of being alive. I was made with purpose and destiny in life, with the understanding of being more than a conqueror.

Even though I had noticeable imperfections, God decided to keep me alive. With actions of joy, I made up in my mind that this situation was not going to win. I used every opportunity of looking for a reason to have joy. I was determined to overcome this obstacle. It could have been worse. I now had more of a reason to prove to God, others, and myself that He is able to do the impossible. Though our outer appearance is not to our likings, the courage and attitude of maintaining joy in the midst of our trial is what makes us beautiful. The inside of what God has made us to be is the antidote of causing change in our lives. We must realize that our beauty comes from within and helps others in being encouraged. We have to pull on our inner strength by believing we are victorious. We should take every opportunity to take the time to notice the beauty of what God is doing in our lives. The joy that we have can not be taken away due to any trial that we face. Beauty is developed in trials. It is the essence that pushes out a fragrance that produces strength, persuading others to not give up. This is why the devil can't steal our joy; it is only offered by our decision of giving it up.

Natural beauty is temporal, but spiritual beauty is everlasting. Godly beauty brings the best out of others while worldly beauty will cause others to fall. We will never know the true beauty of ourselves until we go beyond our outer appearance. True beauty flourishes in challenging times. True beauty will not change in the midst of tragedy but will shine even brighter. "Here's another way to put it: You're here to be light, bringing out the God-colors in the world. God is not a secret to be kept. We're going public with this, as public as a city on a hill. If I make you light-bearers, you don't think I'm going to hide you under a bucket, do you? I'm putting you on a light stand. Now that I've put you there on a hilltop, on a light stand—shine! Keep open house; be generous with your lives. By opening up to others, you'll prompt people to open up with God, this generous Father in heaven" (Matthew 5:14–16, MSG).

My aunt, who was a nurse, came and rushed in. She was the first family member that saw me after the stabbing. Initially, due to the severity of the situation, it was hard on her. My mother and her were close. They were only a couple of years apart. She is the aunt that lived a few blocks away from where the stabbing took place. She was always the one who made sure that everyone was taken care of. She was the type of person that would not rest until she felt assured that everything was going to be okay with whomever she was close to. She came by my bed, holding my hand and rubbing it while staring into my eyes. She was short with words. As I looked at her, her beauty began to take control of the situation. The beauty of her encouragement supported me in receiving strength. She was willing to stand in adversity even when she may have felt she wasn't ready for what was happening in her life. She was willing to do whatever it took to cause joy. She had to push through her hurt and suffering because there was a need that needed to be met. She forgot about herself and concentrated on bringing out joy to live in me. She did not have time to wait on someone else to do what God was leading her to do. The true beauty of who she was came out in demonstration. Her godly beauty gave me that assurance that everything was going to be okay. Her beauty caused life in a dying situation. Her beauty came out of doing what was already placed in her to do. You have that same beauty. We allow fear to stop us from being who we are because we don't like or don't want to accept the situation that is present in our lives. However, someone is waiting on you to take a stand against fear and let what God has already placed in you to breathe and cause life in a dying situation.

A couple of days passed by and my big brother and his new wife had come to see me. He was in the Army's basic training and was called home on emergency leave. My mother had raised us to be very close. She ensured that we kept a tight bond of love for one another. Regardless of the situation, nothing would be able to prevent us from being there. He has always been the courageous one. In my eyes, my big brother was my hero that I looked up to. His presence with me gave me enough courage. I knew he would make sure that I was taken care of. He was hurt and angry and all the above. He had just talked with mom the day before. Moreover, he had no time to heal from his hurt but had to draw strength when it may have seemed there was none left in his being. His little brother was fighting for his life, and he was willing to do whatever it took to make sure that I continued to breathe the breath of life. My breathing caused him to breathe more and his breathing caused me to breathe more. We both knew from within that we both couldn't stop fighting for life. As he encouraged me, I in return, out of gratefulness of him being there, was able to give encouragement, assuring him that my life was not over yet; it was just the beginning of me living life. When he would look at me, I would look back at him beyond my affliction and smile. "A happy heart is good medicine and a cheerful mind works healing, but a broken spirit dries up the bones" (Pro 17:22, AMP). *Affliction doesn't prevent us from smiling, we do.* There is always a reason to smile. Our smiles help others to cope with their trials and struggles in life. Our smile lets the devil know that he didn't cause for us to frown because of the problem. Our smiles are therapy for the way we feel and the way someone else may feel. A smile causes others to see the contentment and helps them believe that everything is going to be all right. *I had a reason to smile because God was with me just like He's with you.* Are you willing to smile in adversity?

Everyone could see the courage through my eyes. This courage motivated others around me to not give up. Those that looked in my eyes saw a fighter. By refusing to give up, it encouraged them to continue on in life. Regardless how bad it may look, we can't be counted out, thinking that it's over. When others see us, they should see the heart of a champion in spite of the trial. We should never have the mind set of being defeated. We can't be defeated, because we are on the winning team of Jesus Christ, and because of this reason, we are blessed. Someone is depending on us to be that strength. We may be the only or last strength of encouragement before it's too late.

Most of my family didn't visit me because it was too hard for them to bear the pain of seeing me in my condition. However, their prayers for me went further than their presence. I believe that God only allowed those who needed to come. I am grateful for the part they took behind the scenes. Therefore, I had no reason to complain and be bitter, but I continued to smile. I was grateful for being alive and having breath to breathe life. Remaining grateful prevents bitterness. Bitterness is like a bad virus. If it's not dealt with properly, it will begin to affect the strength of gratefulness. It will weaken our faith in God, making us believe that everything isn't going to work out. Bitterness will cause our life to be hindered. Bitterness will cause us to forget about what God is restoring and focuses on the hurt that it caused. Gratefulness causes change while bitterness never moves on but continues to go around in circles bitter about the outcome of life. You are alive because God is not finished with you. We all have something to be grateful about; what about life?

I will always cherish my mother, but I have no regrets of her death because I have peace. The after pain that I was about to go through did not matter. I was willing to do whatever it took to overcome this trial. My objective was to live in respect and gratitude of my mother's life through the chance given to me to live. I was determined and focused on life, and nothing else mattered because God was with me. I had given Him my burdens and yokes, and He made them light and easy. Even though I cried, thought a lot, and hurt on the inside, it wasn't unbearable because I gave it to God. He took my sorrows and pains and changed them into blessings. *He reminded me that I was made beautiful just like you.*

Will Through Pain

As God began to heal me from the inside out, there were some challenges that I had to deal with. The initial start of the healing process was the doctors taking the bandages off my body. As the doctor approached me, he told me that this might hurt some. The doctor began to talk to me so I would be more into the conversation versus what he was about to do. He talked to me about various type things, and I started laughing. I had a big smile on my face, acting as if I were out of the hospital with some friends on the street corner. As I laughed, I had forgotten about the fear of pain that I might go through. Then immediately, he ripped the bandage off from my side, and instantly there was an excruciating sharp pain that ran through my whole body. The tape felt and sounded like Velcro separating from my skin. Great pain shot through my body. I didn't have any way to release the pain outwardly because my vocal cords weren't healed enough to release the trauma I was dealing with at the time. I opened up my mouth and tried to yell as loud as I could, but nothing came out. My screams were locked within; it was a silent yell that stayed within me. Only I could hear the screams and struggles I felt. The expression on my face was of someone that could not explain what was wrong, but you could tell whatever it was it hurt really badly. Furthermore, I had to use my body to release the anguish. I squirmed left to right, sticking my chest up in the air while the doctor was holding me down. My legs were kicking back and forth but limited because of the nurse holding my legs down. The pain shot up and down my body with great throbbing on my side. Beads of sweat poured down my face. The pain lasted for about fifteen to thirty minutes. Even though the bandage was off my skin, it felt like it still was on my side for a few days. Needless to say, I lost some of the feeling on my side because of it. *Healing is produced through faith in action.* There is a two-part process of healing: Firstly, there is *covering of the wound.* If a natural wound isn't covered properly, it will cause the wound in never being properly healed. Eventually, the wound will get worse than it was because of it producing possible infections and disease. We also should be concerned of our spiritual wounds being properly covered. We lose our covering in God when we begin to doubt what He can do in our lives. While going through the healing process from a wound in our life, God ensures that we are properly protected. God covers the cuts of our wounds so it will not get infected by the enemy. The covering lasts until it has formed enough scar tissue (faith in God) to defend itself from the infection of doubt. Faith in God is the source of nutrients that build the self control of withstanding any tribulation. It will form a defense of protection from doubts.

Secondly, God will *remove the bandage from the wound*–when it's time to take off a natural bandage, it will not be fully healed. It's only healed enough for it to build enough protection for the wound to breathe. Removing of the wound is not dictated off of our feelings or the wound being fully healed. God removes the bandage from wounds when he sees enough faith built up in our lives during the tribulation. Yet, the wounds are not fully healed; the wound must breathe. In God's timing, He allows for our faith in Him to develop, giving us room to mature. This is why it is important for us to walk in our healing because walking in healing is another form of maturity.

The doctor began to unveil the bandages with scissors that was over my head. He took everything that needed to be taken off to go into the next phase of healing. He was getting me prepared for the next phase of surgery. As time went on, God continued to heal me rapidly. While the doctors performed their duties, they were still puzzled as to how I was healing so fast. I began to receive more strength in my neck: I was able to keep it up without it falling to the side. One day, I felt like it was time to walk to the restroom because my legs started feeling stronger. I got sick and tired of urinating in a pan as I lay in the bed. It had been a week or two; I felt like it was time to start walking again. I stood up on the bed and pushed my legs to the edge, allowing them to hang toward the ground. I stopped thinking about it, and I just did it. Before I knew it, I was standing. I was a little hesitant, but I kept standing, then I started to walk toward the restroom. My steps were as baby steps, but I refused to doubt that I could remain standing on my own strength with my legs. I had gone too far to give up now. The nurses were looking at me with concern, ready to catch me if I were starting to fall. They stood by the side, believing without any interference. It took a few minutes, but I made it to the restroom.

I set my heart on making it to my destination, and I just did it. God has a plan for your life. Don't be afraid to take a step of faith toward your purpose. Faith in God will alleviate fear. If my heart had fear in it, I wouldn't have made it to the restroom. We have to stop second-guessing what God can do in our lives because of trials. In order for us to make it toward our purpose, we must set our heart on it and be courageous, believing that we can make it. When I was finished, I made it back to my bed without any injuries. God gave me the willpower to endure the pain by succeeding in standing.

"So if you're serious about living this new resurrection life with Christ, act like it. Pursue the things over which Christ presides. Don't shuffle along, eyes to the ground, absorbed with the things right in front of you. Look up, and be alert to what is going on around

Christ—that's where the action is. See things from his perspective" (Colossians 3:1–2, MSG).

We must look beyond the state of the situation at hand and set focus on what God has proclaimed over our lives. *We can do anything God sets in our hearts to do.* There is no opposition that is powerful enough to stop the purpose of our lives in being fulfilled. It's time to pursue and go after it.

Meanwhile, the investigators had proceeded with the autopsy and finalized the report. My mother had been cremated, and it was time for the funeral. I begged and pleaded to go to her funeral, but my family and the doctor wouldn't let me go. The doctor said that it would be too dangerous while going through recovery. I was very saddened because of the verdict, but I remained encouraged. My family also told me that my last moment with my mother should be of something pleasant and not of my mother in a casket bringing back the memory of the tragedy. I had no actual reason why I wanted to be there, but I just felt like I needed to be there to see her for the last time. Sometimes we allow our feelings to drive our decision making process without consulting God first. It will cause us into being offended when we don't get our way. The Self always thinks that it should happen a certain way. However, *we must learn how to wait on God until He gives us the approval.* Whatever we do, we should not resist God. *God knows exactly what He's doing.* God has us in the specific place he needs us to be at for proper healing to happen. When we get out of position, anything can happen. *We must learn how to accept when God says, "No."*

It had been about three weeks by now, and God continued to heal my body and my vocal cords. After the doctor checked the healing of my throat, he approved me to start eating out of my mouth again. Until then, my food was liquidated in a bag and oozed down the tube through my nose to my stomach. It felt very icky going down, but I needed it for nourishment. The nurse began to pull the tube out of my nose. The tube moved up through my stomach, past my chest, up my throat, and out of my nose. The process took only a few minutes. I thought I was going to throw up. I started off eating soft foods that were something that a baby would eat. I ate things like Jell-O, pudding, mashed potatoes, ice cream, etc, and I drank lots of water and juices and ate lots of ice. After being able to eat again, there was no turning back. It felt so good to use my mouth again. Moreover, God continued to heal me rapidly even though there still was more healing to be done.

"But those who wait upon God get fresh strength. They spread their wings and soar like eagles, they run and don't get tired, they walk and don't lag behind" (Isaiah 40:31, MSG).

Have you ever been in a waiting position? In some situations, waiting is not the first option. When waiting seems to be more of a challenge in facing difficulties, we would prefer that it sped up. However, waiting is essential in our development and maturity. To wait means holding out while moving forward in service.

We hold out by not giving up in the place of life we're in. While waiting, as we receive strength, we must continue to move until the trial is finished. *Moving forward produces more strength in causing us to look beyond the obstacle and being able to look at the end of it before getting to the destination.* Yet, the trial is not fully complete; we must learn how to take notice of what God is doing in our lives. God is manifesting a miracle in the midst of all the odds.

Breathe

"The Spirit of God made me what I am, the breath of God Almighty gave me life! And if you think you can prove me wrong, do it" (Job 33:4–5, MSG).

Breathing is not difficult at all. Inhale, and then exhale. Until death, we continue to breathe. Our very existence is based upon our breathing. However, in life I have found out that there were times when breathing became very difficult. Nevertheless, I made the choice to continue to breathe. Why choose to breathe when situations seem as if they aren't getting better? Why breathe when life seems to be so hard and there is no way out? Why breathe when society has written you off? For the few minutes that it took you to read this paragraph, during the time that you have read this part of the book, have you noticed you are still breathing?

Even though trials of life seem to be stale and suffocate our desire to live, it can't stop us from breathing. However, in order to win this battle, it will take for us in concentrating breathing. Suffocation occurs when we lose heart of our purpose because of the trial we face. However, we must make the choice to fight and persevere through our emotions and what it may look like naturally. Eventually, the suffocating of life will break off because we didn't give up. Furthermore, because we have accepted the choice to breathe, victory occurs immediately. Through acceptance to breathe, it produces courage to breathe again and again. God has placed a mechanism in us to maintain victory through life's struggles of suffocation. Who says we can't breathe even though things aren't always so wonderful? It's a challenge, but if it wasn't, we would take breathing in life's challenges for granted. We must choose the choice to breathe regardless how and what we have to face. Sometimes we have to remind ourselves we are still alive by simply stopping for a minute and taking a deep breath and then exhaling. Inhale the freshness of God by allowing Him to change the situation and blow out all the negativity of the situation.

The process of breathing out my mouth took more time. Even though I could eat food and drink liquids, I still couldn't breathe out of my mouth. My breathing came through a tube that was surgically placed in my neck called a trachea. The trachea that was in my neck carried all the mucous in my body. It was imperative that I cleaned the tube that came out of my trachea on a daily basis. The trachea was sustained by a mere piece of string wrapped and tied around my neck which was similar to tying a shoe string. I had to get comfortable with sleeping on my back versus on my stomach. In order for me to rest at night, I had to make sure that a compressor was covering my trachea. The mucous stayed moist as long as the compressor covered the trachea as I slept. If the compressor fell off during the night, it could cause the mucous to dry up and become hard, which could cause suffocation while sleeping.

As my neck was healing, I had to experience approximately ten surgeries. There were times after surgery when my throat would be very sore. Swallowing was one of my harder tasks because of the pain that I felt after surgery. My only comfort was eating lots of ice to subside from the pain. There were tests that I had to take that would monitor the healing of my throat. I was told to practice those tests frequently because the exercise was to get me used to breathing normal again. They gave me a tube with a plastic ball at the bottom of it that I had to blow in. By blowing into the tube, it would cause the doctor to see how much air I could push out of my mouth. Initially, by blowing with all of my might, the ball only moved a hair length high. It was frustrating and at times would eventually make me feel as if I would never be the same again. I never had problems breathing before, but now I couldn't breathe; I physically and spiritually had to fight for every breath that I took. If I stopped fighting for breath, it was likely that I would never breathe normal again. However, I refused to be discouraged by what I saw. I kept trying! What I saw naturally was not greater than what I believed spiritually. I wouldn't allow what I had seen to enter into my mind thinking negative thoughts. I continued to believe that I would breathe out of my mouth once again like before. I didn't have time to think about what others might have said to discourage me. I just believed! Every success of healing that I noticed, I held onto it. Remembrance of what God had already done gave me purpose to believe that full recovery was on its way. The expectation grew as the healing began to manifest into reality. Deep down inside I knew that I would be healed. During the process of blowing through the tube, I was able to blow from a hair length to a half inch. I knew even more that it was a part of God's will for me to breathe. Moreover, I refused to allow anything to stop me from progressing forward until I received total breathing.

Have you ever started something but stopped at the middle or three-fourths of completion? Why? Was it because you got tired, you settle for the easier choice, or did you just give up on *you*? I faced the same opportunity just like anyone else going through a trial. Trials should be referred to as opportunities to prove we are capable of overcoming them. My trial was an opportunity to prove that I could breathe even when others said I would never again. We give up too easy at times. When we should keep pressing, sometimes we tend to give up. Nevertheless, don't stop breathing and give up on the God ability that's in you. You have what it takes to continue to breathe in life's challenges.

A trial is another opportunity to put our faith to the test. Quitting never can cause for us to have a greater faith in God. As a matter of fact, giving up constantly will eventually kill all hope, purpose, desire, and ambition in life. Situations will happen. The challenge is not the situation that we face. Moreover, the challenge is within. We have to fight and push through our fears, hurts, failures, discouragements, etc. Trust God no matter what happens. Know that the victory is already ours; but we have to cause victory to be manifested in our lives. Whatever holds us back starts internally within us and will eventually cause for us to begin to blame others for our shortcomings. We have to be careful in blaming others for what we go through. Trials we face are only there in order for us to recognize the opportunity we have in falling more in love with God. Our acknowledgment toward Him causes Him to perform another miracle in our lives. We must have faith even if it may not seem easy to do while going through difficult times. If everything were so easy then we would take our life for granted. Our life is worth fighting for. However, because we have ups and downs in life, it keeps us remaining fresh in God. Faith in Him causes new thoughts, new ideas, and new ways to do things. Some of those things that God shows us are not going to make a lot of sense, nor make us happy all the time, but remember that God knows what He is doing to cause success in our lives. So if I must choose not to quit that I might live, then I must make that choice knowing that everything else that comes with that choice will fall into its place. If I had stopped trying, I would have killed my purpose, will, and destiny for my life. Daily, people are killing their purpose, will, and destiny because they feel like it's simply too hard. Today make a choice to breathe and don't let the fight for it stop you!

Alone with God

"Look at me. I stand at the door. I knock. If you hear me call and open the door, I'll come right in and sit down to supper with you! (Revelation 3:20, MSG).

Night after night I laid in bed thinking about my life. Family and friends were gone, and the nursing staff was minimal. There were many times I felt so alone. I felt trapped. The walls seem like they were closing in on me. There was no place I could run and hide. I would feel discouraged when no one else was there with me. During the day, I was confident and was an encouragement for others. I had gone through so much within a day. I was worn out by night. *If only I had someone to talk to during those times of feeling alone,* I thought.

Loneliness is a false deception of thinking and believing no one is there with us. Loneliness works with our emotions. Emotions can get the best of us if we let it. Emotions can manipulate us into thinking that we need someone in a physical body more than we need God who is Spirit. Loneliness causes one to operate in doubt and fear and tries to influence us in doing whatever it takes to receive comfort the wrong way. Fear of what man can do enters in making us feel vulnerable. Loneliness tells us that no one is there, but we must remember that when no one else is there, God is still there. In order to combat loneliness, we have to acknowledge Him as being there with us. When acknowledgement of Him is lost, the time with God is replaced with things of loneliness. Without acknowledgement of Him being there with us, it opens up the gate of all manner of negativity of doubts to come in. He stands and waits, eagerly anticipating for us to let Him in our heart. God is patient and will long suffer for us. He understands the pain and hurt that we go through. He will never get tired and leave us alone. He will come in, sit down and listen to our heart. He will then speak into our heart to empower us for our purpose in Him.

Eventually, I realized that I wasn't really alone, God was there all the time, waiting to commune with me. Initially, I was hesitant in opening up to God because I was afraid. I was losing my blessing. This was the best time to express my sorrows and for Him to speak into my heart. I didn't know how to act or what to say. However, I had to understand that God was there to help in areas that I couldn't help myself. He made sure He spent time with me alone away from distractions. When no one else was around and it was quiet, I could feel His presence hovering over the space I laid. God was right there, ready and desiring to enter in my secret places of hurt and pain. He shaped my character into more of His likeness in preparation for my future. While I was all alone, His presence remained in the room, protecting me from ungodly thoughts of giving up hope, nightmares about the burglar stabbing me, and discouragements of never overcoming the scars of my life. But God gave me the assurance that I could sleep and get rest. The next morning, I felt reenergized and prepared for the upcoming day.

While I was in surgery, He was on watch. Every cut from surgery and touch was orchestrated by the hand of God. The doctors could have made a mistake, but God would not let them. God gave me the strength to stay positive even though some had doubted that I would fully recover. God wiped my tears when I cried and embraced me when I felt alone. God proved Himself as my hero. He stuck with me through it all. I understand now that God had a relationship with me. He was closer to me than anyone could ever be. He honored my cry and He encouraged me when I was weak. It was in those quiet places when I was able to reach past every hindrance and get to God. I was alone with God and He heard my distress, sorrows, and pains. He was the "I AM" in my life. He comforted all my pain with His touch. It gave me that inner peace that does not come from anyone else but Him. After spending those times with God, I just knew that everything was going to work out. He constantly ensured that every-thing was going to be alright.

"I have strength for all things in Christ Who empowers me [I am ready for anything and equal to anything through Him Who infuses inner strength into me; I am self-sufficient in Christ's sufficiency]" (Philippians 4:13, AMP).

We have to allow God to be our sufficiency. God will increase our trust in Him by our willingness in letting Him in our lives. Openness toward Him is the passage He takes to heal the brokenhearted. God goes into the secret places of our heart that no one else can reach. There are times when God wants us only to Himself. He can't minister to our needs of healing when there is so much commotion and distractions happening all around us. However, God waits for His time with us daily. *Great peace comes in quiet places.* Too many people around us during difficult times cause more of a hindrance than help. There are times when we must be alone only with God. God yearns for a deeper relationship with us. He wants us to open up without hesitation. Communication should come from the heart. Talking with God is beyond verbal commu-nication, but it is also being able to speak out from the heart internally. Words to God while being alone are more intimate and secret because no one knows or can hear the conversations. The one-on-one conversation renews and restores in preparation for the next day. It will fully prepare for whatever is to happen because of the time spent alone with God.

Our time with Him is vital and shouldn't be taken

lightly. He sets up daily appointments for preparation for the trials we face. During these appointments, He infuses inner strength with enough confidence and fortitude in being ready to overcome the next hurdle of life. He desires daily relationships with us in order to continually pour out His empowerment to be ready for anything. Opening up to Him by talking, listening, and trusting in what He says is how we receive this power. He is the medicine that is needed for healing from the spirit of loneliness. When alone with God, it gives us the time to be able to be re-strengthened. He transforms our thought patterns from sorrows and discouragement into confidence and perseverance that everything will be all right.

God heard my cry because I was desperate and focused on living life. God will honor our prayers when we are desperate, solely depending on Him. Whatever it takes to gain life, we must be able to surrender any and everything to live. We must get to a point of saying, "It doesn't matter anymore. What matters is that I am with God, because with God in my life, I am able to live." If we could stay in a state of believing that all power is in His hand, our prayers would be answered more often. Our prayer should be in desperation versus obligation. We can not live unless God gives us the strength to live. Even when it seems as if no one is there, we cannot accept what the devil is trying to do in our lives. There is too much purpose, destiny, and will of God that is still in us that has not been pushed out yet. We must accept life! Tell the devil no and say yes to God. Our victory in those times of being alone is by keeping God in our heart and denouncing loneliness. *Our actions by accepting God being there is the "Amen" in our lives.* We must know that we are coming out victoriously. We can't allow anyone to cause us to believe different from what God has told us. *If God has spoken it, then that settles it. We are coming out of the mind set of loneliness and will accept life.*

Confidence!

"In Whom, because of our faith in Him, we dare to have the boldness (courage and confidence) of free access (an unreserved approach to God with freedom and without fear)" (Ephesians 3:12, AMP).

In order to have confidence in God, can we agree by saying we must first have faith? Faith is the access to enter into confidence. Faith in God is the evidence of the unseen without depending on what we see. Faith is what we believe to be truth, but then we have to be able to apply our faith by moving into confidence. In order to move into confidence, we must first believe. It is possible to have faith without confidence. However, without confidence in God, we are not moving; we are just believing and standing still, allowing life to pass right by. Our hindrance is not having faith, but it's having confidence in what we have faith in. Confidence is the movement of faith. After praying and having faith to be healed by God, we must now move in confidence in our healing from God.

Because I prayed by faith, I believed that God would heal me. I believed that I had to move in my healing. Moving into healing is operated by confidence. I pushed myself into doing things that the Spirit of God was leading me to do through faith. As I began to receive strength in my body to walk, I began to minister to other people who were in the Intensive Care Unit. Even though I couldn't talk, I did not allow the ministry that was in me to prevent it from coming out and being a blessing for someone else's life. My ministry was in smiling and serving those that might need a drink of water or juice. I would also stand in front of those that were lying on their bed of affliction and pray that God would heal them. There was much opportunity for ministry. Without a shadow of doubt, I knew God was with me. I wanted to bless someone else with that same assurance. Without complaint, I walked by faith and moved in confidence. I wasn't concerned about my situation because I had assurance everything was okay. That same assurance gave me the desire to share with someone else. I used what was in me to cause change. The change was having confidence that I could help others when I, too, was receiving help.

If we trust Him, He will use what He has already placed in us to make a difference. Be willing to cooperate with the will of God in your life to be a blessing for others. *Stop making it difficult and stop contemplating and do it the way God has been telling you to do it.* What God has placed in us is able to bless someone else in being confident of what's in them. We have to be able to use what God has put in us until He reveals other gifts that are locked within us. God will not unlock other gifts until we move in the ones that are already unlocked. The gift of God that is placed in us cannot be stopped by trials. However, it will be stopped by our choice. The gifting of God may not operate the way that we think it should be, but we must accept how God desires to use us; it may be simply a smile.

If we believe by faith in God, we must move by faith in the confidence of God to get the work done. Our faith in God moves us in the confidence of God. It directs us toward our purpose in Him and reveals to us why we are alive. God has every intention to use us to help someone else. Regardless if we are poor, rich, black, white, etc, we have work in us that needs to be completed before we die. Accept the opportunities that God places in your hands to do before it's too late. No more turning away, but it's now time to take hold of life to produce more life in someone else.

"And I am convinced and sure of this very thing, that He Who began a good work in you will continue until the day of Jesus Christ [right up to the time of His return], developing [that good work] and perfecting and bringing it to full completion in you" (Philippians 1:6, AMP).

There is unfinished work that needs to be completed. There is no time for excuses; we must use what we have to be able to get the work of the LORD done in our lives. Our work in God is helping others around us to be encouraged. We have no reason to feel that we are useless. God has already made the difference in our lives. The main reason why we are alive is because there is someone that we have not met that needs to be encouraged by the testimonies that God has allowed us to go through. Be assured that God has everything in control! Walk by faith, and move in confidence!

A Mother's Sacrifice

"No one has greater love [no one has shown stronger affection] than to lay down (give up) his own life for his friends" (John 15:13, AMP).

At times, we allow the pain of situations in being a permanent hindrance without taking the time to understand its purpose through it. We prefer to ignore it when we don't understand why and act like it's not there or try to erase the memory of pain it caused. If we're not careful, it will hinder our life in where God wants to take us and keep us in that hurt place. However, a sacrifice of love has to be made for life to be given. With sacrifice comes power.

I wish my mother were still alive. However, I had to accept the reality of the death of my mother instead of believing that I was going to wake up and it would all go away. Her death caused me to live. A mother lives with the desire for their children to move further in purpose. She lives life as an example for her child to be able to be persuaded in such a way that they may choose righteousness.

At times, we don't like the reality of sacrifice because it's not appeasing. The sacrifices that are made of those we love are challenging to accept. Sacrifice will produce change in our lives. We can not only allow the change to be so traumatic that we can't continue in fulfilling our purpose in God. If we are not careful, the act of sacrifice will cause us to be bitter. We can't take for granted why sacrifice occurs in our lives. Moreover, if it hadn't been for the sacrifices in our lives, our relationship with God wouldn't be as strong. Sacrifices are meant to bring us closer to God. When sacrifices are made, God will replace the sacrifice with a greater anointing in living. These situations of sacrifice occur to bring the best out of us. Additionally, sacrifices are meant to birth new life.

The purpose of my mother's death was so that I would live life. I never looked at it that way until I realized that the scar of losing my mother was what gave me the motivation to stay alive. I used her sacrifice as strength for life. Now I can be grateful today because her sacrifice produced life in me. Yes, at times I get discouraged, distressed, want to quit, and wish that she was still alive, but the reality is that her life has to live in me. Because of her sacrifice, I have a conviction to live and reach my purpose. It keeps the passion of living and prevents the hindrances from driving me into death. I refuse today to walk away from my calling in God. I will fulfill the promises that are destined for my life.

My mother's example pushed me to Jesus Christ. There was a love that she couldn't give that only God could give. Her sacrifice has given me the drive to carryout where she stopped. I have no regrets because the tragedy of losing my mother has provided the change in me gaining Jesus Christ in my life.

I have had the opportunity to know my mother for eleven years. I live in tribute of my mother's sacrifice. Because of my mother's life, I have an unquenchable push toward my purpose in God in recognition and acknowledgement toward her life. Losing my mother was considered a tragedy. However, I've refused to allow the tragedy to be the last memory of her living. I have learned how to live through the tragedy. Oftentimes, we allow the tragedy to kill our purpose in life because it seemed to be so traumatic. We must learn how to change our tragedies into triumphs. I've learned that tragedies lose their sting through perseverance of not giving up on breathing life. As difficult as it may sound, we must continue to breathe life, and it will eventually heal the pain of the tragedy and turn it into triumph. The tragedies are meant to be stepping stones toward our purpose.

Sometimes we ask the question, "Why?" Why did I have to lose my mother? What did I do to deserve this? Why not someone else instead of me? Is this a part of God's plan for my life? I had to realize that these were all legitimate questions. I desired more of my mother's love, teaching, and instruction. I felt like I was just beginning to understand my mother's love. Moreover, I was entering into another phase of my childhood, and I needed her to be there with me. As in some households, my mother was my father and my mother; she was two in one. She was the only one I had that I knew to call on for help. My mother was the world to me. I would have given up anything just to be able to feel her touch once again. Her love, her laugh, and her correction—there was nothing like it. She was a great influence in my life. She was willing to give up her life so that I might live. She sacrificed her ambitions, goals, and desires that I might achieve mine. I live my life not only for myself but also in tribute of my mother. The life that I live must be in recognition and honor for her; I can't allow her death to be in vain. I have to prove to the world that God allowed her to die that I may live. I live as a testimony of my mother's sacrifice. My mother's death will not stop me from living life.

> Dear God, I thank you for the opportunity of having a mother. I have no regrets, but I cherish every moment that I have had with her. You working through her allowed for me to be the man of God that You have called for me to be. Though the trials that I have faced in the past were challenging, You made away for me to survive. I realize there is nothing on this earth that is so hard that You can't help me through. I will not walk in defeat but live in victory. You have given me the strength to be more than a conqueror. I stand and continue to live life

because of You. I am honored and privileged to be able to say that I had a mother. In Jesus' name, Amen!

Overcoming
the Statistic

"We don't want you in the dark, friends, about how hard it was when all this came down on us in Asia province. It was so bad we didn't think we were going to make it. We felt like we'd been sent to death row, that it was all over for us. As it turned out, it was the best thing that could have happened. Instead of trusting in our own strength or wits to get out of it, we were forced to trust God totally—not a bad idea since he's the God who raises the dead! And he did it, rescued us from certain doom. And he'll do it again, rescuing us as many times as we need rescuing" (2 Corinthians 1:8–10, MSG).

Society has set statistics that show the numbers of those that have been birthed in hard neighborhoods never come out alive or make a difference by changing the outcome of what they have experienced while growing up. The pressures of life seem to be so hard and so traumatic. How can one go through such violence, pain, and hurt and still live? Society attempts to advertise it as being literally impossible to overcome the environment in which we are birthed in. The thought is *once a victim always a victim*. It is already predicted that they will eventually be another statistic of what tragedies do to people.

For example, women that are drug addicts and pregnant, will cause for their child the additional complication to fight against being a drug addict from the time of birth. During the time of conception, the child will go through withdrawals of not having drugs any longer as its source of satisfaction. In order for this child to overcome the stronghold of addiction to drugs, it has to withstand the taste of the drug. It's not the child's fault that it is addicted to drugs. The child never had a choice. This was just the life that was given to the child. This child is labeled as a dope fiend before it is old enough to understand what had taken place. The child, according to statistics of the environment that the child grows up in, will be labeled as a victim of its generation before it is old enough to understand what happened. The child will grow up having to fight through the statistic. The child will have to choose what lifestyle it's going to follow: a defeated lifestyle, accepting the fact that he/she is what society has made them to be, or a lifestyle that will edify and make a difference in their own lives as well as others.

People are going to talk. But we can't always listen to and accept the negative things people say about us as if it's true. Turn it around. Use those things as positive fuel to move forward. If someone says, "You will never amount up to anything; you should just throw in the towel; you are a loser," use it as fuel and make the negative words into lies. What ever we do, we can not surrender or retreat to the enemy's plan. We have to fight through it. In order to win this battle, we have to struggle through hardship to produce change. Struggling builds character, attitude, endurance, motivation, etc. Many times, our downfall is how we go through our struggles. Moreover, fear of going through the trial is what causes us to stand still in defeat. This type of fear is due to not wanting to face the reality of the trial. Fear is an attribute of selfishness; it is only concerned about one's self versus others. However, there is strength within us all that is greater than any attack that we may face on earth. Though the trial may seem horrific, we must take our stand against it. The sight of the trial shouldn't be our reason of defeat. God has given us the ability in pressing through our trials without losing strength in the middle of the situation. Moreover, we press to move on, without turning back. We have to be convinced that we are able and capable of overcoming our trials.

Before I went through this tragedy, everyone in my family was being killed in some manner. They were being taken out one by one. It was a generational curse.

Generational curses are like leaches that will suck and suck until the thing is bone dry, taking all of its substance of life in it away and leaving it useless and in ruins. This generational curse was the spirit of murder. In each generation, someone else was being killed. The devil had devised a plan to wipe out the family seed through murder. His purpose was to stop the work of ministry in my family. If the devil could kill our seed, our future existence would be destroyed. Our children's children would have never been afforded the opportunity to live life. The devil understands this and desires our seed of purpose. He will do whatever it takes to attain it. He is willing to do and use anything he can to defeat us. He knows and sees the potential of greatness that we have. Because of this reason we are considered a threat to his kingdom.

A generational curse will last as long as we allow it to last. My mother and I were the next victims on the devil's list to destroy the ministry within the family. Once I overcame the stabbing, I was faced with the challenge of the statistic of being considered someone that was destined for defeat. Maybe I should have died and given up hope because of the tragedy, or maybe I should have tried to avenge the burglar who did this to my mother, or maybe I should have become unforgiving in my heart forever. This is exactly what the statistic will make us think. However, in order to overcome the statistic, I had to refuse hopelessness, revenge, and un-forgiveness. Instead, I had to rely on God's assistance because I wasn't able to overcome the statistic on my own. I had to give God my burdens and accept His ways. In order for me to remain freed from the statistic of being defeated, I had to combat against the hurt, the scars, and fears. We have the power to break any stronghold in our family's lives by facing it, without being intimidated by its roar of seeking destruction. Furthermore, our life is important. God's plan in our lives is to assist in causing others to live by our pressing through our trials. Someone is depending on us to face these challenges so they can use them as an example to remain victorious in their own lives.

Joy is Strength

"But none of these things move me, neither count I my life dear unto myself, so that I might finish my course with **joy,** and the ministry, which I have received of the LORD Jesus, to testify the gospel of the grace of God" (Acts 20:24, KJV).

Have you ever felt like there was a way out but couldn't find it? As you searched and tried to go every place that you thought would be an escape route, you ran right back into a dead end. At the beginning of this journey, it was an adventure because it was something new and fresh. Eventually it became a burden versus a blessing. The joy of the journey became too tedious and made us feel discouraged. What happen? The joy of facing new challenges was not a joy anymore. It became a hindrance. It wasn't turning out the way we expected. It was envisioned to work out a certain way. However, what happens when it doesn't turn out the way you expect it to? Do you give up and run away? Do you make excuses why you can't keep moving forward? Do you reject any help that others are trying to give? Do you allow yourself to get frustrated and aggravated to the point of it changing your character into being negative?

Though we go through various trials in our life, it can bring joy. We have to learn how to feed into our spirit to keep ourselves positive. There is nothing that is able to steal our joy. We lose it by freely turning it over to the trial. We have to maintain the joy while we're going through the trial. Take time to say "thank you" to the LORD. Remember it could have been worse. When was the last time you honored God in your trial? Know that God will never take you through something unless it was for your development and growth in Him. This is just another opportunity for you to express how much you love Him and give you the conviction to refuse the situation from influencing you by doubting Him. The more we keep joy within our hearts, the more the trials won't be able to trip us up. God has given us the power to change the outcome of any trial in our lives by simply thinking on things that are true. What we think will eventually come out in our speech. If we think, *I am not going to die in this situation but live, I am a conquer, I will breakthrough my challenges, and I am capable to withstand the fiery trials that come my way,* then it will counterattack the negative feelings that may occur.

Just because trials come our way, who says we can't have joy? "A *merry heart* maketh a cheerful countenance: but by sorrow of the *heart* the spirit is broken" (Proverbs 15:13, KJV). There is strength in having joy. Joy restores the desire and willingness to remain focused on our purpose. It will bring into existence new ideas and a fresh attitude of dealing with situations. Without joy, it will be difficult to be led by the Spirit of God. It will prevent spiritual fruit from growing in our life. It will be a constant battle from within. Without joy, it will cause a bitter heart. The attitude of overcoming will be replaced with the mind set of blaming others and fault finding in others. Our outlook on joy shouldn't be when everything is going well. It should be our lifestyle.

Trials would be easier to face if we would let go and let God handle them. Joy is always within reach; yet, temptations may come. Stop making it so hard to do. Take a deep breathe and then blow it out and smile. God has everything under His control. You already have the victory. It's time to start moving in it. It may take more effort in order to maintain joy in certain times of life.

We have to believe. Though we have scars, our life is blessed. Our present can change our future. *Our present is the gift that God has placed in us to achieve joy in life whether if it's during good or bad times.* When we present our gift in action, it not only causes joy in our lives, but it also touches other people's lives all around us. In other words, we must be willing to offer joy even in the most difficult times. We have to learn how to use joy as strength in times of trouble. When we represent joy, we are opening up and revealing who we are without shame and fear. Anytime a gift is offered, it normally brings joy and celebration. Our gift is invaluable, and no one can put a price on it because it is sacred unto God. When we present who we are, the motives behind it should cause ministry to assist change and make a difference.

A Living Testimony

"And they have overcome (conquered) him by means of the blood of the Lamb and by the utterance of their testimony, for they did not love and cling to life even when faced with death [holding their lives cheap till they had to die for their witnessing]" (Rev 12:11, AMP).

I have had some trials and some victories, but through it all I have matured in ways that are not common to man. God has brought me closer to His bosom through the years. Over 20 years of my natural life, I am still here and still standing on the promises of God! Even though the scars are even now present, they are not there to discourage me, but they are there to remain as a testimony. I use my testimony as an assistance and assurance that God is able to make what seem impossible, possible. It reminds me of how God delivered me out of the devil's hand. This book is my purpose, will, and destiny. I live through the cuts, hurts, and pains to be an example for someone else. I am alive today because I gave up on doing it my way and laid down my life in God's hands, believing that He was going to put me back together again. I had to let go and let God take control 100 percent. I am a living testimony of what God is able to do if we trust Him.

The devil seeks to prevent us from remembering what God did to get us this far in life. A testimony can not be a part of our lives unless we utilize it to live life. The cuts are experiences that God allows us to go through so we would have the opportunity in proving to ourselves and others that He is greater than the opposition that we face. The reason why it seems as if we are going around in circles is because we have to let go. Letting go is the process of putting our trust in God without any reservations of thinking He can't fix it. Our testimony should always have the same foundational message regardless of the situation we face. The foundation of any testimony should be expressed when we have released it out of our hands and have given it to God that, "Nothing is too impossible for God to handle." The truth of the matter is God is still performing miracles today. Moreover, miracles are happening everyday. This trial, just like others, allowed God to perform a miraculous healing that no one could take any credit for but God. All my cuts, hurts, sorrows, pains, etc, have been compiled into a testimony that produces praise and thanksgiving toward God. Once the trial was over, it didn't seem as difficult and challenging because God was with me. Testimonies produce life when we continue to move on faith in action.

Trials cause more of who we are to come out in demonstration. However, through the demonstration of the trial we must guard our hearts so we don't get discouraged because of what is happening in our lives. By doing this, it will cause a testimony to form in whom God has called us to be. Our testimony is our specialty of who we are in Christ. We are what God has made us to be through the trials that we have faced. We are living testimonies waiting to burst out issues of life. Though trials cause scars, God has equipped us with inner strength to overcome all of them. In order to produce victory in trials, the scar must produce healing. When healing comes, shame and disappointments leave; they cannot occupy the same space. Through hurt, pain, and sweat, strength is developed in being able to live life with the scars that we have dealt with. Jesus came, died, and was resurrected for us, that through Him, we might have life and have it more abundantly. Why? Because we have something special to give out that only we can express through the life we live. The easiest way to move on is to accept that the scar can't prevent us from expressing who we are and whose we are. We belong to the LORD of LORDS and the King of Kings, Jesus Christ! Moreover, friends, family, and enemies may try to persuade us in thinking different, but we must never take what God has done in our lives for granted. Be persuaded that God is working things out for our good. Refuse any negative or doubtful words others may say. Constantly feed your spirit by remembering we are living testimonies.

Victim to Victor

According to most people, it was assumed that I wouldn't live through this tragedy. I was supposed to lose my mind, get into crime, go to jail, and live life carrying on with an attitude of defeat. I was labeled a victim, never overcoming the tragedy. My direction should have been toward ruin and bitterness because of the traumatic life-changing experience caused. My life was considered over. The case was closed, and I would have been forgotten within one or two days. God stepped in right on time and kept the case open that I may live. But I had to prove to myself, others, and the world that I wasn't a victim of hopelessness, but, rather, a victor of elation and hope.

In the world's eyes, we are labeled as victims before victors. In life, our greater challenge is being able to remove these labels that are placed on us because of the situations that we face. Labels can only be removed by the help of God. Initially, it may seem easier to give up and accept the label that was placed on us. However, we will lose out of what He desires to do in our life. We can't be discouraged because the process is done differently than we thought. God's promises are not temporal but permanent. We have to continue to trust and not forget that He is going to do what He said.

At times it's hard for us to accept what happens in our lives. Most of the time, we would rather not even look at it because it reminds us of the situation. The mindset is, "If only I could get rid of the remembrance of the scar." The scar will remain and continue to live. Moreover, scars are meant to be remembered. We can't be naïve, acting as if we didn't go through this trial which produced a scar in our life and hope that it would go away. If the scar isn't going away, then that means we have to use the scar for what it is worth. God allowed the scar to be produced in order for us to see and remember that He performed a miracle in our lives. That same miracle is capable of fabricating other miracles as we continue to keep the scar alive. Scars are meant to produce more life. The scar can't be ignored because it's where our gift is originated. Our scars are meant to be used as strength, remembering that God is able to do the impossible.

The scar of the situation can either die in us, or it can live and change our lives. None of the potential that God had placed in me would have ever been able to be pushed out of my life if I would have accepted the negative words spoken over my life. The stabbing was meant to kill every aspect of my life through me accepting my life as being destroyed. I could have allowed the brutality to place a stigma of living out my purpose. I would have been alive living purposeless without any joy—"a dead man walking." The enemy can't kill the purpose of a child of God unless it's surrendered in defeat. We can't be defeated because God gave us the spiritual power to overcome the enemy. "Little children, you are of God [you belong to Him] and have [already] defeated and overcome them [the agents of the antichrist], because He Who lives in you is greater (mightier) than he who is in the world" (1 John 4:4, AMP). It doesn't matter that I went through struggles, hardships, pains, and long sufferings because I continued to remember that I was alive because of the grace of God. God assured me that He still had life in me that He wanted to push out of me to cause life into another person's death situation. I am a victor because I didn't stop living. I am a victor because I can look at the scars and not be ashamed. I am a victor because I realize God has everything under control. My face might have been severely bruised, and I might not have been able to talk for a while, but God would not allow me to stop living because I put my trust in Him. I am a victor because of God. I did not have the physical strength or stamina to overcome this evil thing that happened in my life. My edge was God living inside of me.

Today, you might be going through a situation that is causing you to feel like giving up. Though these feelings are coming, it is still your choice to either say, "I quit," or to say, "I am not giving up this time!" I encourage you to not give up and remember God can fix the impossible in your life. God will keep and take care of you. All you must do is believe, trust, and rely on God to be your light to see yourself through the passageway. Don't allow what you see naturally to cause fear to rise in your life, but have faith by putting it into action. I put my faith into action by walking by faith, and because of that walk, it caused healing. Your faith walk will cause a disruption to the devil's plan. I could have easily lived as a victim, but I refused to. I'd rather walk in victory and help those that are victims and convince them into changing their minds into being victors. We must remember whatever confession that is made, that's what you are. We kill our dreams and desires by losing our confession. Anytime that we begin to doubt, we must continue to remind ourselves that we can make it. We can't allow anything or anyone to change our confession. I encourage you in not giving up on your goals and ambitions due to a mental or physical injury that left a scar. We are not victims but are victors. The scars that are in our lives are testimonies that give us fuel to move forward.

A Prayer for Life

Dear God,

Touch everyone that reads this book. Allow your anointing to fall fresh upon them. Send forth healing and determination to fulfill their purpose in You. God, I pray that no one is left out, but bless those that are in need of strength in living through their scary situations. Let every word that was written down on this paper be anointed to cause resurrection power to stand even though they have scars in their lives. Let these words touch those that are brokenhearted, discouraged, and feel like giving up. Let them be able to face and press through their challenges of their scars. Search out their hearts and give them understanding why it is important that they face their scary situation. Those talents and gifts that You have placed in their lives, let them come to life through their scar. I pray that these scars that have been a part of their lives cause them to walk in purpose in remembrance of Your grace in their lives.

I pray against the attacks of the devil that has bound some in the mind, making them think that their birth was a mistake. I tear down the spirit of fear that creeps in the middle of the night. I rebuke the spirit of quitting because of challenges that they may face. I speak against every negative word of death spoken into their life, making them believe that it's not worth it anymore. LORD, I ask that you continue to remind them of their worth; they are special in Your sight. As they face obstacles, give them hope and assurance that everything is going to be alright. Let them not regret when they are challenged in standing for righteousness. Give them peace in the times of stormy trials. With every step they take for victory, let them feel and know that You are right there with them. Let them keep vigilant watch over their heart; so out of it will follow issues of life. I pray that they will see how colorful their life really is in You. Let them continue to express their joy by being courageous, being ambitious, and be unwavering in overcoming their challenges. Remind them in remembering that their life isn't over but that it has just begun. I pray that it will charge them into being persuaded in You, knowing that You are right there with them through the thick and the thin of life.

Moreover, God, allow this book to cause challenge and motivation in people's lives that surpasses all understanding. Destroy the yokes and remove the burdens so they will be free to live in abundance in You. Free their mind of thinking negative and being in doubt. I proclaim victory in conquering life's scars and let it sound off in their actions. Today, let them begin a new way of breathing life that it will help many. Let them remember that they are *Scarred, for Life. In Jesus' name, Amen!*

Endnotes

1   Copyright (c) 1984, *Daily Breeze*, All Rights Reserved Record Number: 0000033838